CITY CRITTERS
Raccoons
by Betsy Rathburn
BLASTOFF! READERS
1
BELLWETHER MEDIA • MINNEAPOLIS, MN

Blastoff! Readers are carefully developed by literacy experts to build reading stamina and move students toward fluency by combining standards-based content with developmentally appropriate text.

Level 1 provides the most support through repetition of high-frequency words, light text, predictable sentence patterns, and strong visual support.

Level 2 offers early readers a bit more challenge through varied sentences, increased text load, and text-supportive special features.

Level 3 advances early-fluent readers toward fluency through increased text load, less reliance on photos, advancing concepts, longer sentences, and more complex special features.

★ **Blastoff! Universe**

Reading Level

Grade
K

Grades
1–3

Grade
4

This edition first published in 2025 by Bellwether Media, Inc.

Library of Congress Cataloging-in-Publication Data

Names: Rathburn, Betsy, author.
Title: Raccoons / Betsy Rathburn.
Description: Minneapolis, MN : Bellwether Media, Inc., 2025. | Series: Blastoff! Readers: City Critters | Includes bibliographical references and index. | Audience: Ages 5-8 | Audience: Grades K-1 | Summary: "Developed by literacy experts for students in kindergarten through grade three, this book introduces raccoons in cities to young readers through leveled text and related photos"– Provided by publisher.
Identifiers: LCCN 2024035386 (print) | LCCN 2024035387 (ebook) | ISBN 9798893042207 (library binding) | ISBN 9798893043174 (ebook)
Subjects: LCSH: Raccoon–Juvenile literature. | Urban animals–Juvenile literature.
Classification: LCC QL737.C26 R38 2025 (print) | LCC QL737.C26 (ebook) | DDC 599.76/32–dc23/eng/20240810
LC record available at https://lccn.loc.gov/2024035386
LC ebook record available at https://lccn.loc.gov/2024035387

Editor: Christina Leaf Designer: Gabriel Hilger

Printed in the United States of America, North Mankato, MN.

Table of Contents

What Are Raccoons? 4
Raccoons in the City 10
Raccoons and People 18
Glossary 22
To Learn More 23
Index 24

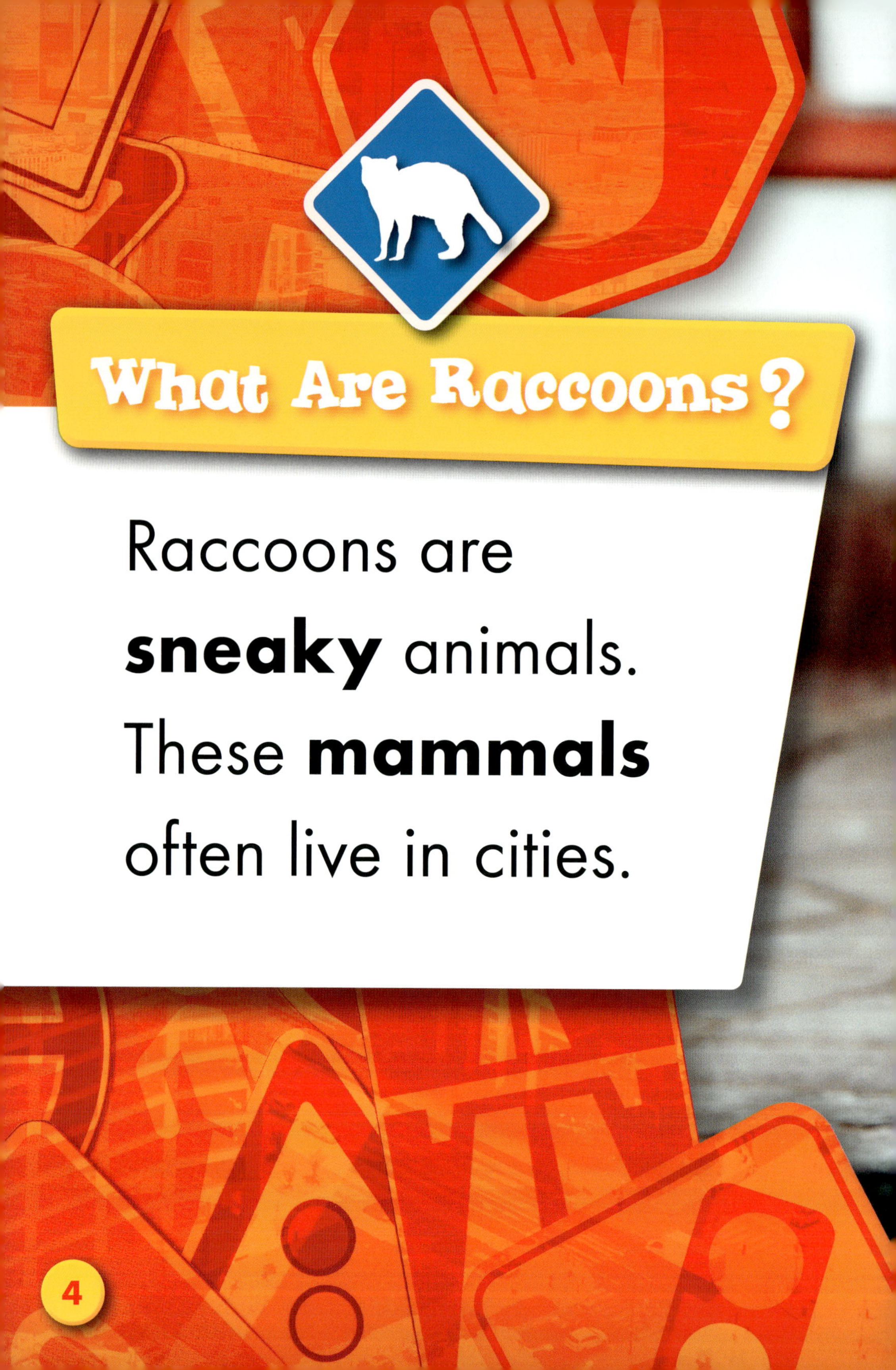

What Are Raccoons?

Raccoons are **sneaky** animals. These **mammals** often live in cities.

Common City
Raccoon
northern raccoon

Raccoons have thick bodies with gray fur. Their faces have black masks.

mask

They have long,
striped tails.
Their front paws
hold items easily.

paws
tail

Raccoons in the City

Raccoons sleep high in trees. They also make **dens** under porches or wood piles.

Raccoon Homes
trees
under porches
under wood piles

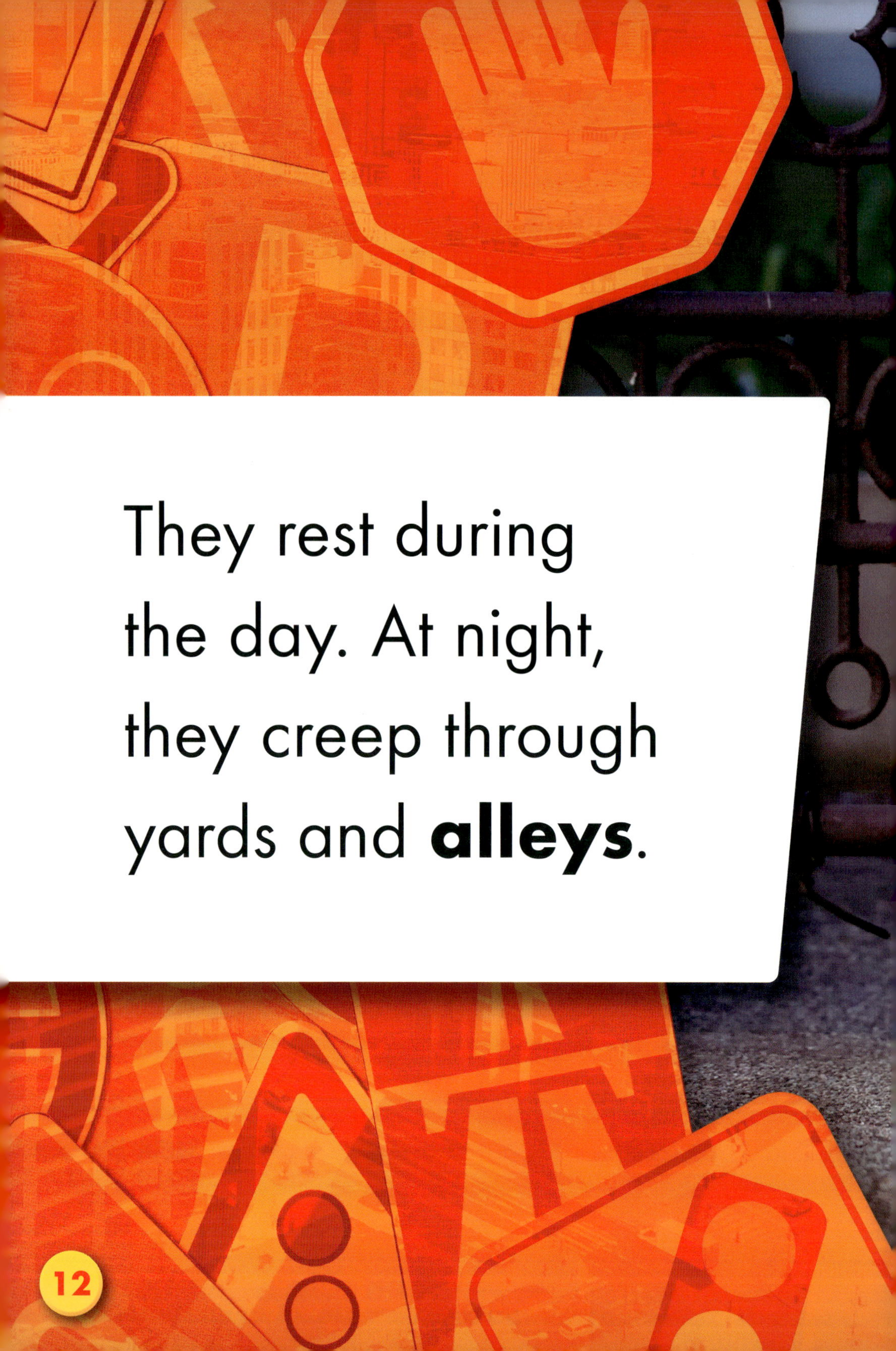

They rest during the day. At night, they creep through yards and **alleys**.

alley

They search gardens and trash cans for food. They eat almost anything!

Raccoon Food
bugs
fruit
trash

They look and listen for **predators**. They race up trees to escape danger!

predator

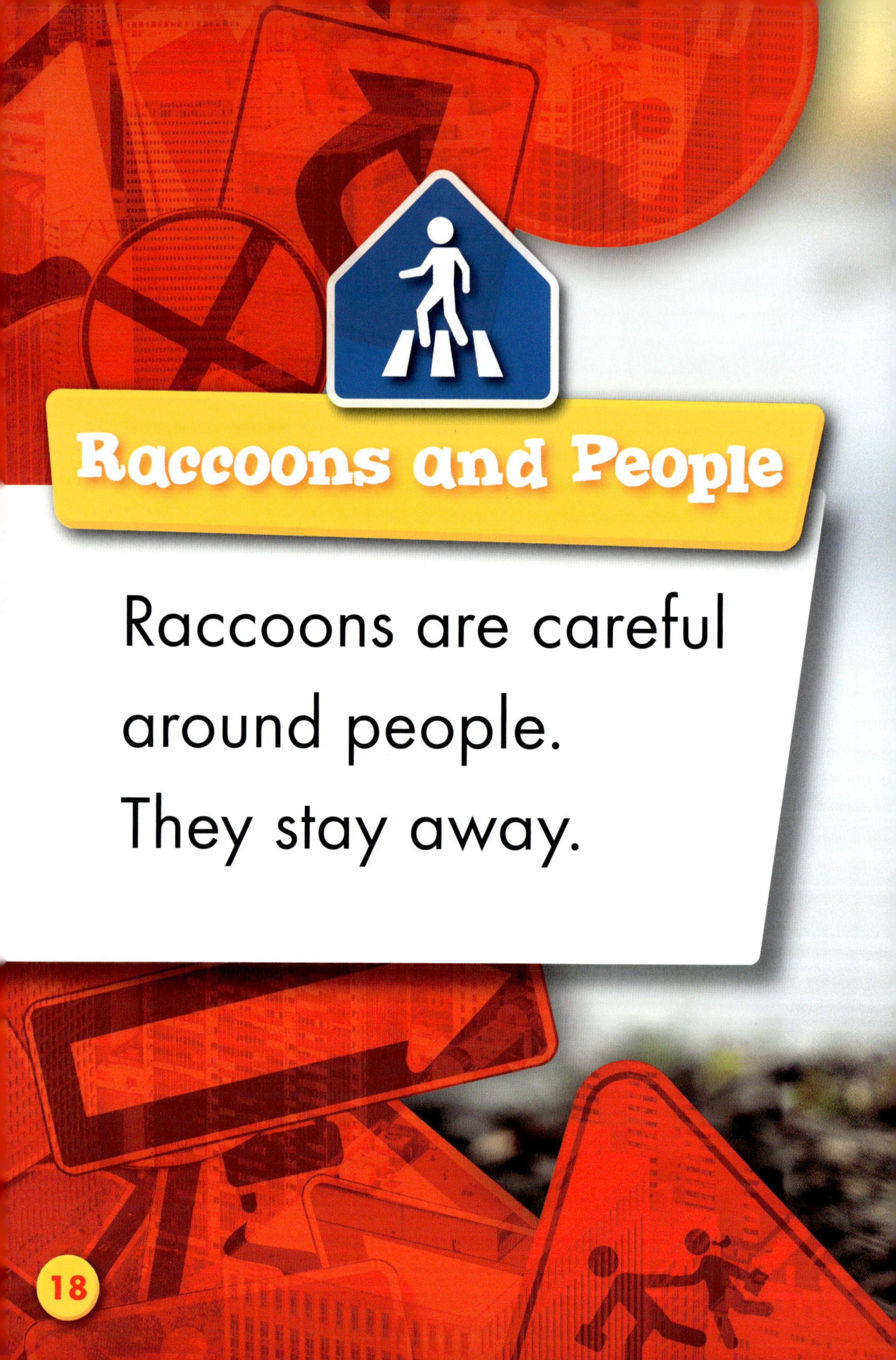

Raccoons and People

Raccoons are careful around people. They stay away.

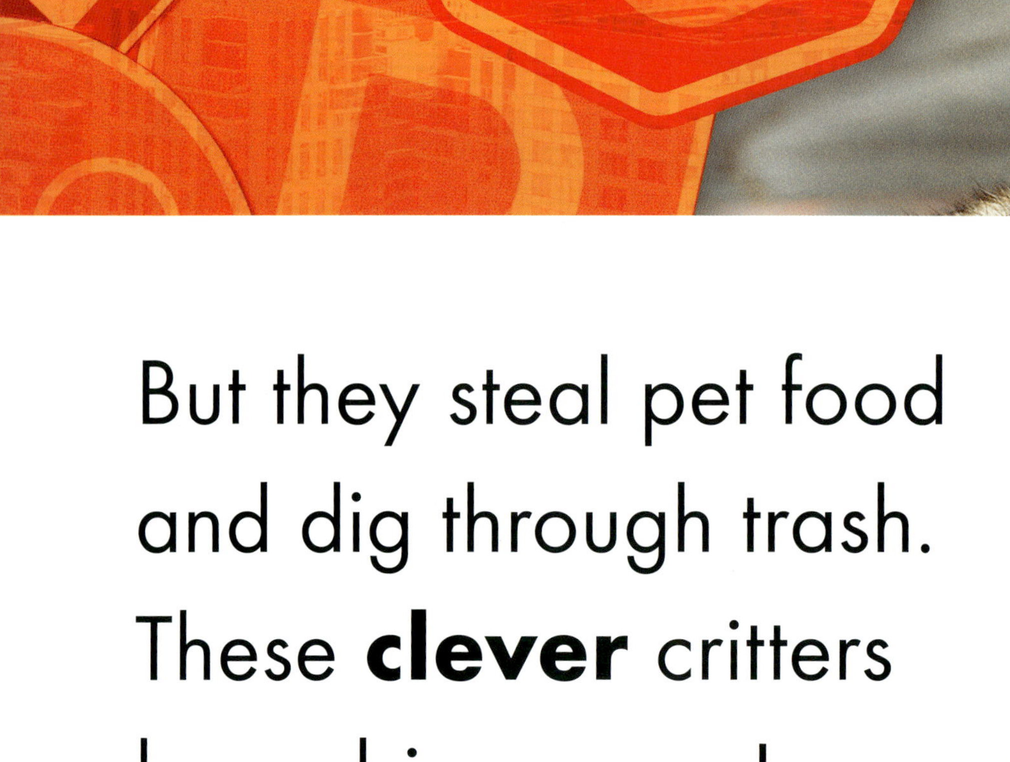

But they steal pet food and dig through trash. These **clever** critters leave big messes!

Glossary

alleys

pathways between the backs of buildings

mammals

warm-blooded animals that have backbones and feed their young milk

clever

smart or quick to learn

predators

animals that hunt other animals for food

dens

sheltered places

sneaky

doing things in secret

To Learn More

AT THE LIBRARY

Carney, Elizabeth. *Animals in the City.* Washington, D.C.: National Geographic Kids, 2019.

Riggs, Kate. *Raccoons.* Mankato, Minn.: Creative Education, 2023.

Scheffer, Janie. *Raccoons.* Minneapolis, Minn.: Bellwether Media, 2025.

ON THE WEB

FACTSURFER

Factsurfer.com gives you a safe, fun way to find more information.

1. Go to www.factsurfer.com.
2. Enter "raccoons" into the search box and click 🔍.
3. Select your book cover to see a list of related content.

Index

alleys, 12, 13
cities, 4
colors, 6
common city raccoon, 5
day, 12
dens, 10
eat, 14
food, 14, 15, 20
fur, 6
gardens, 14
homes, 11
mammals, 4
masks, 6, 7
night, 12
paws, 8, 9
people, 18
porches, 10
predators, 16, 17
sleep, 10
tails, 8, 9
trash, 20
trash cans, 14
trees, 10, 16
wood piles, 10
yards, 12

The images in this book are reproduced through the courtesy of: Eric Isselee, front cover (raccoon), p. 5 (northern raccoon); Jon Chica, front cover (city); GlobalP, p. 3; jon chica parada, pp. 4-5, 20-21; magda michalska, pp. 6-7; Jeff Kingma, pp. 8-9; MyImages_Micha, p. 9 (inset); Harald Schmidt, pp. 10-11; Wirestock, p. 11 (trees); AEWD, p. 11 (porches); JasonOndreicka, p. 11 (wood piles); Devonyu, pp. 12-13; Krikof971, pp. 13 (alley), 22 (alleys); Tom Middleton, pp. 14-15; UtahTransplantDoc, p. 15 (bugs); Kristina Savelieva, p. 15 (fruits); Siyanight, p. 15 (trash); bukharova, pp. 16-17; JamesChen, p. 17 (predator); Coffee Uncle, pp. 18-19; KyleBedell, p. 22 (clever); mb-fotos, p. 22 (dens); lavin photography, p. 22 (mammals); eumates, p. 22 (predators); Joe Duquette, p. 22 (sneaky).